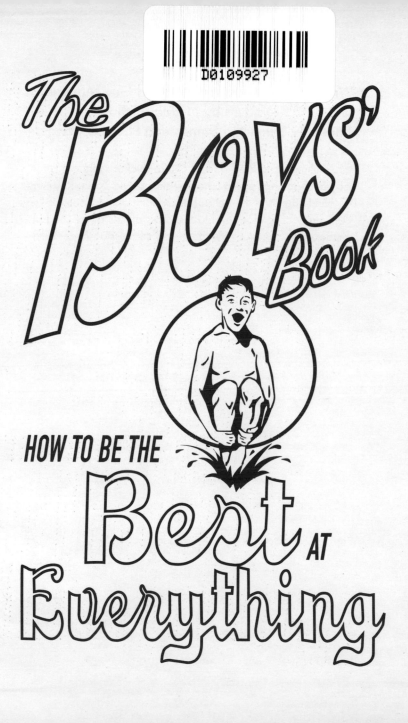

The BOYS' Book

HOW TO BE THE Best AT Everything

Written by Dominique Enright and Guy Macdonald
Illustrated by Nikalas Catlow
Edited by Samantha Barnes and Philippa Wingate

Grateful thanks to Ellen Bailey; Claire Buchan; Jamie Buchan;
Toby Buchan; Agnieszka Chojnowska; David Bann; Ray King;
Dr. John L. Breen of the School of Oriental and African Studies,
University of London; and to the press offices of the London
embassies of Greece, Sweden, and the Russian Federation.

The BOYS' Book

HOW TO BE THE

Best AT Everything

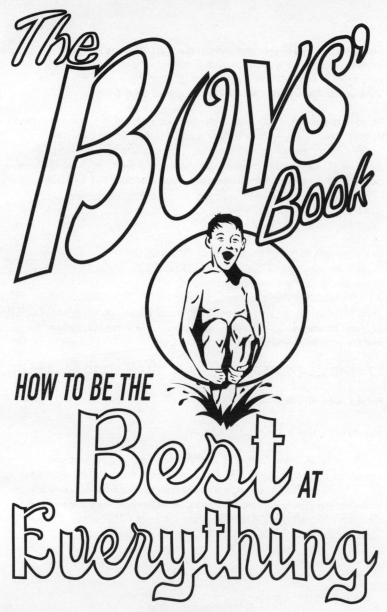

SCHOLASTIC INC.

New York   Toronto   London   Auckland   Sydney
Mexico City   New Delhi   Hong Kong   Buenos Aires

ISBN-13: 978-0-545-05799-8
ISBN-10: 0-545-05799-X

Text copyright © Buster Books 2004, 2005, 2006
Illustrations copyright © Buster Books 2004, 2005, 2006
Cover illustration by Getty Images.
All rights reserved. Published by Scholastic Inc., 557 Broadway, New York, NY 10012, by arrangement with Buster Books, an imprint of Michael O'Mara Books Ltd. SCHOLASTIC and associated logos are trademarks and/or registered trademarks of Scholastic Inc.

12 11 10 9 8 7 6 5 4 3 2   8 9 10 11 12 13/0

Printed in the U.S.A.   40

This edition, March 2008

The Boys' Book: How To Be The Best At Everything is a revised and expanded edition of How to Be The Best At Everything, first published in 2004 by Buster Books, an imprint of Michael O'Mara Books Limited. It also includes material from Children's Miscellany: Volume One, Children's Miscellany: Volume Two, and Children's Miscellany: Volume Three published in 2004, 2005, 2006 by Buster Books.

CONTENTS

NOTE TO READERS

The publisher and authors disclaim any liability
for accidents or injuries that may occur as a
result of information given in this book.

To be the best at everything, you'll need to use your
best common sense at all times: always wear
appropriate safety gear, stay within the law and
local rules, never hesitate to ask an adult for
assistance, and be considerate of other people.

HOW TO DO AN OLLIE

This technique is the basis for most other skateboarding tricks. It allows a skater to jump over an obstacle, or onto a step or low wall, while the board appears to stick to the skater's feet. Always wear a helmet and knee and elbow pads when you're skateboarding.

1. As you skate, place your back foot on the tail (back) of the board, and your front foot halfway between the nose (front) of the board and the tail.

2. Crouch down in readiness to jump. Push down on the tail with your back foot.

3. Now straighten your legs, effectively jumping into the air. The downward force on the tail will make the board come up with your front foot.

4. As the board rises, slide your front foot toward the nose. Then, with that foot, push down on the nose.

5. Lift your other foot to allow the tail to rise as the downward force is applied to the nose.

6. The board will be level as you reach the peak of the jump. Then gravity takes hold, and you and the board come down.

7. As you descend, bend your legs to absorb the impact.

HOW TO FLY A HELICOPTER

The spinning rotors on top of a helicopter allow it to take off and land vertically. It can also hover, spin around, and move forward, backward, and sideways. This means that, as a helicopter pilot, you can fly and land almost anywhere.

1. On your left-hand side there is a lever called the collective pitch stick. This adjusts the main rotors so that the helicopter can move up and down. It also has a twisting handle that controls the engine's speed. By increasing the lift and the engine speed at the same time you will make the helicopter rise off the ground.

2. Directly in front of you is a joystick called the cyclic pitch. This makes the main rotor tilt so that it can pull the helicopter backward, forward, or sideways. Move the joystick in the direction you wish to travel.

3. At your feet are pedals that control the tail rotor. Use these to spin the helicopter in any direction.

HOW TO PERFORM A CARD TRICK

Here's a card trick that is
guaranteed to fool everyone:

1. Before you perform the trick, you
need to make a trick card. Cut the
king of spades in half and glue it
to the front of the 10 of diamonds.
Position it halfway across the 10
and slightly tilted to the right, as
shown here.

2. Next, take three cards from the
deck — your trick card, the 5 of hearts, and the jack of clubs.

3. Fan out the cards as shown below. Make sure the jack
is completely hidden behind the 5 of hearts, so only the

10 of diamonds, the king of
spades, and the 5 of hearts
are showing.

4. Show the fan of cards to
your audience. Then close
the fan. Turn your hand
over and fan out the cards
again, holding them
facedown.

5. Ask someone to pick out the king. They will probably
pick the middle card, thinking it is the king. It won't be the
king; it will be the jack.

HOW TO SURVIVE IN SPACE

If you're very rich, you could go to space on vacation. The other way to get to space is to become an astronaut, and an astronaut must be the best at everything.

You have to wear a spacesuit while traveling on the space shuttle, but on the space station you can wear ordinary clothing. You'll spend time on board the space station growing plants, making crystals, and performing experiments in near-zero gravity.

You will need to exercise frequently to minimize the loss of bone and muscle mass caused by weightlessness. Gym equipment is provided. During your free time, you can send e-mails home, play cards with fellow astronauts, and admire the view of Earth.

You will eat in the galley. The food is in containers attached to a tray, which is in turn attached either to you or to a wall (otherwise your meal will float away). The meals themselves are not made up of tablets, though — you get real food just like at home.

You will sleep in bunk-style sleeping quarters or, if there's not much room, in sleeping bags. These, of course, have to be attached to a wall or they will float around and you'll wake up in another part of the station.

As there's no washing machine on board, you will need to take a great deal of clothing with you. Dirty clothes are washed using condensation and soap in plastic bags, one article of clothing at a time!

The toilet is fairly similar to those on Earth. A steady flow of air moves through the unit when it is in use, carrying waste to a special container or into plastic bags. The plastic bags are then sealed. (Some of the waste might be returned to Earth for laboratory analysis.)

To wash, you will have to take a sponge bath using a wet washcloth and soap that doesn't need to be rinsed off. You can't take a bath because the water will float around. This is very dangerous, as it could short-circuit electrical equipment.

As for brushing your teeth — that can be a challenge, too. You will have to swallow the toothpaste or spit it into a washcloth.

You may have to perform space walks to complete your mission. This will involve getting into a spacesuit, which has been made to withstand flying debris and to protect astronauts from dramatic temperature changes (from −212°F in the shade to over 248°F in the hot sunlight). The spacesuit has a pressurized atmosphere, a source of oxygen, a means of removing carbon dioxide, a temperature regulator, some protection against radiation, and the means to communicate at all times with ground control and/or the space station.

After going through depressurization procedures in the air lock, you'll step out. A crew member safety tether will keep you completely attached to the space station.

HOW TO LOSE YOUR HEAD

You will need a chair and a table to sit at, with your homework set out on the table. You must be wearing a large shirt with buttons down the front and a collar.

1. Sit down on the chair. Unbutton your shirt and pull the neck of it up around your head. Rebutton the top three buttons behind your neck, with your head poking forward.

Make sure that your shirt is firmly tucked into your pants at the back. Shape the collar of your shirt (which is now behind your head) into a neck-shaped circle.

2. Still sitting on your chair, duck your head under the table. With your free hand, make sure that the front of your shirt collar is at least level with the tabletop, preferably above it. Make sure, too, that the collar is still in a roughly neck-shaped circle.

3. Now put your elbows up onto the edge of the table. Pick up your pen in one hand, look busy, and wait for people to come in and see how your homework has made you lose your head.

Think of other times when you can make a headless appearance. It can be really funny at mealtimes, or at a friend's party.

HOW TO MAKE A ONE-SIDED CIRCLE

The one-sided circle, or Möbius strip, named after a German mathematician, is a loop with only one surface and one edge. Impossible? Well, here is how you make one:

1. Cut a strip of paper (try to keep the width even so that you have a long, thin rectangle like the one shown here). To make sure you tape the loop the right way, write A on the top right-hand corner, B on the top left, C on the bottom right, and D on the bottom left as shown here.

2. Hold the two ends in your hands, give the strip a half-twist by turning the end marked D and C upside down, then tape together the ends, A to D, B to C. Now you have your loop, like the one below.

A Möbius strip

3. Now take a pen and, starting at any point, draw a line along the center of the strip, continuing all the way around until you reach the starting point of your line. You'll have drawn a line on both sides of the loop — but without lifting your pen or crossing any edge, which means the paper has only one side.

4. Take a highlighter and color the edge of the strip. When you reach your starting point, you'll find that both edges are colored, which means the strip has only one edge.

5. Now, with scissors, cut the Möbius strip along the central pen line that you drew earlier. It does not, as you'd expect, fall apart into two separate loops — instead you now have a single, larger, one-sided loop!

6. Draw a central line around the resulting loop and cut along it — can you predict what will happen?

HOW TO FIGHT OFF A CROCODILE

Crocodiles are efficient killing machines. They might seem slow, but they can move very quickly in the water and leap out suddenly and at great speed.

1. The best way to avoid a crocodile attack is to maintain a safe distance from any area where crocodiles might be lurking.

2. If you're standing near a lake and a crocodile springs from the water toward you — run. And keep running for at least 50 feet.

3. If the crocodile has clamped its jaws around one of your limbs, do not try to pull yourself free. Crocodiles' jaw-closing muscles are incredibly powerful, and it is almost impossible to pry them open. Instead, try to reach for a stick or anything else to use as a weapon, and hit its sensitive nose repeatedly and poke it in the eyes. (A man once actually managed to make a crocodile let go of his arms by biting its nose as hard as he could.) It might just back off, but crocs are quick, and you'll have to keep fighting it off until you can run to safety. Yell for help as you battle the crocodile.

Crocodiles are generally wary animals that prefer to keep their distance from other large animals. Still, the best way to prevent an attack is to constantly maintain a respectful and safe distance yourself!

HOW TO SWIM FREESTYLE

So you want to ditch the doggy paddle? The fastest and most impressive-looking swimming stroke is the freestyle (also called the front crawl).

Body and head: Your body should be straight and streamlined, with no arms and legs sticking out and your hips in line with your shoulders. Keep your face in the water, looking at the bottom of the pool. Move your head only when you need to take a breath. As you swim, try to keep all of your body close to the surface of the water.

Legs: Use these to keep you up and maintain your balance, as well as to propel you along. Try to make long, fast kicks, ensuring that the whole length of each leg is moving up and down. Bend your knees slightly and splash only a little with your feet. Try counting to six quickly and kicking your legs alternately in time with this.

It is important to keep your legs close together (but, of course, not so close that they move as one).

Arms: These are your main source of power. Stretch one arm in front of your head as far as you can, close to the surface of the water, letting your shoulders and hips follow. Then slice your hand down through the water, thumb first, splashing as little as possible. Keep your fingers together, forming a shallow scoop to help pull yourself through the water. As you bring your arm down, bend your elbow and pull your hand toward your feet, your fingers following a path down the middle of your chest and stomach. When you bring the arm back up to repeat this stroke, try to lift your elbow out of the water first.

Keeping your hand near the water's surface and close to your body, move it forward to the start position in front of your head.

The second arm should follow the first so that it is about to go down in front of you as the first is coming up. With some practice, you'll slip into the rhythm of the alternating strokes, your hips and shoulders rolling slightly to the left or the right as you stretch each hand forward.

Breathing: Your face is in the water, so you must remember to turn your head when you want to take a breath. Turn it as smoothly as you can, leaving the side of your head resting in the water. An effective method is to turn your head to the left to breathe when your right arm is outstretched and to bring your head around to the right to breathe again as you stretch out your left arm.

You should now be able to kick, pull, and breathe. Keep your legs kicking all of the time and your arms following each other. Get into the habit of breathing regularly, every two, three, or four arm strokes. And try to avoid splashing too much — it's not cool or professional.

HOW TO PLAY A BLADE OF GRASS

1. Find the biggest blade of grass you can — the taller and wider, the better.

2. Press the sides of your thumbs together, with the nails facing toward you.

3. Place the blade of grass between your thumbs, so that it runs vertically.

4. You will now be able to see a strip of grass in the gap between your knuckles and where your thumbs meet your hands.

5. Blow through the gap. If you don't hear a whistle at first, adjust your lips and the grass, and keep trying.

HOW TO BE A VIP

If you are very important, you must know very important people. So impress your friends by greeting any stranger you pass by in the street who looks as though he or she might have some kind of status. Quite often the person will say "Hello" back, thinking that you're the child of someone they know. "Who's that?" your friends will ask. "Oh, that's the famous painter so-and-so"; or "That's Henry So-and-so. He owes me a favor — that's why he pretended not to see me. I'm going to have to call him"; or "That was DJ Dingbat. He's always asking me what CDs to buy." And so on. Don't overdo it — your friends will catch on. But get it right and they'll be full of respect.

HOW TO TIE THREE ESSENTIAL KNOTS

Different knots are used for different purposes. Here are three really useful knots that you can use all the time.

Reef knot: This is used to tie one rope to another if the ropes are of the same thickness. This knot is also useful for tying bandages, because it lies flat. When tying, always remember: "left over right and under, right over left and under." When you have finished, pull the knot tight.

Sheet bend: If you need to tie two ropes together that are of different thicknesses, you should use a sheet bend. When you have finished, pull the knot tight.

Clove hitch: This knot is used to tie a rope to an object. Sailors might use a clove hitch to tie their boat to a dock.

HOW TO AVOID BEING EATEN BY A BEAR

To avoid a bear in the wild, keep a clean camp. Bears can smell food and garbage from a long way away. Stay away from mammal carcasses. Never pet a bear cub.

If you are unlucky enough to be approached by a bear, stand your ground. Make yourself look bigger by holding a jacket over your head. Shout at the bear. If the bear makes contact, drop to the ground and play dead. Lay on your stomach and clasp your hands behind your neck. Do not move until you are certain the bear has left the area.

HOW TO PLAY THE TOILET PAPER ROLL

A kazoo is one of the world's simplest musical instruments. To make one, you will need: a cardboard tube (from a roll of paper towels, plastic wrap, foil, or toilet paper), waxed paper, a rubber band, scissors, a ruler, a pencil, and colored pens or paint.

1. Start by decorating your tube (this is optional, but who wants to be seen playing a toilet paper roll?).

2. That done, cut a square, 5 by 5 inches, of waxed paper.

3. Place the waxed paper over one end of the tube and secure it with the rubber band.

4. Hum or sing into the open end. The waxed paper will vibrate to give a buzzing effect that enhances the sound you make.

HOW TO SPOOK YOUR FAMILY

Could your house be haunted? It could be, if you have anything to do with it!

Every morning, your family comes downstairs to find that the table has been set — and that one chair is pulled out, and there's coffee in the cup at that place, as though someone had been sitting there and had just gotten up from the table moments before — but there's no one there.

Things move. However often your mother puts that vase of flowers on the mantelpiece, the next time she comes into the room, it is back on the table. And that's not the only thing that moves. Furniture, too, appears to have moved by itself during the night.

The dog whines and scratches at the never-used door to the basement (or spare room, pantry, etc.). Nobody knows why, except you — you know his favorite chew toy is hidden behind it.

At night, when everybody is asleep, lights go on, found in the morning by whoever is first to get up. (Make sure no one hears you get up in the night.)

One particular door seems to always open by itself (the one to which you can attach a bit of string without it being spotted).

Clothes that have been left lying around all appear neatly folded in a pile. Some clothes disappear from one drawer to reappear in someone else's drawer.

Other things seem to have moved. The cans in the cupboard are stacked, their labels swapped, and the eggs in the fridge are hard-boiled. And the chocolate keeps disappearing!

Footsteps, music, and talking are heard from another part of the house, but there's no one there. (Keep whatever machinery you use to record and play the sounds well hidden.)

HOW TO GIVE MOUTH-TO-MOUTH RESUSCITATION

Mouth-to-mouth resuscitation could save a person's life. Many types of injury can cause someone to stop breathing, and if this happens, a person has little time before they suffer brain damage or death. Don't practice on a person who is breathing — it can be dangerous, so use a doll.

1. Check to see if the injured person is breathing. If he's not, call 911.

2. Check to see if there is any blockage in the air passages — including his tongue. Use your fingers to remove any obstruction you find.

3. Look for signs of breathing. If he is not breathing, put him on his back and loosen his clothing.

4. Tilt his head back by lifting his chin. Hold him firmly by the chin and by the top of the head. Make sure his airway (the passage in the throat) is clear.

5. Hold his head and pinch his nostrils shut between your finger and thumb.

6. Take a deep breath, and then seal your lips firmly around his mouth. Breathe out steadily into his mouth. His chest should rise (if it doesn't, it means there's a blockage that needs to be removed — quickly). Remove your mouth, watch the chest fall, and then blow into his mouth again.

7. Check for breathing, and check the pulse by placing your first two fingers on the underside of his wrist.

8. Continue the pattern of blowing into the injured person's mouth and watching his chest rise and fall for 12 breaths. Check again, and if he hasn't started breathing by himself, continue until he does or until help arrives.

9. If he's started breathing, you'll need to put him in the recovery position. Place the arm closest to you straight out from the body. Lift and bend his far arm at the elbow, resting it against the near cheek. Grab and bend his far knee and then, protecting his head with one hand, gently roll him toward you by pulling his far knee over and to the ground. Stay close until help arrives.

HOW TO FOOL YOUR FRIENDS WITH TOOTHPICKS

Freak out your friends with this simple but sneaky trick.

1. Look carefully at this diagram. Arrange four square-ended toothpicks in exactly the same way.

2. Ask your friends to make a square by moving only one toothpick. They will really struggle.

3. Move the left-hand toothpick a little to the left and, in the middle of the toothpicks, a sneaky square will appear. It is important to have the blunt ends of the toothpicks in the middle of the square.

HOW TO EAT IN A FANCY RESTAURANT

DO

Put your napkin on your knees right away.

Start with the outer silverware and work your way in with each course.

Finish your mouthful and wipe your mouth with your napkin before sipping water.

Say "Excuse me" if you need to leave the table.

DON'T

Lean your elbows on the table.

Eat french fries with your fingers.

Eat with your mouth open.

Yell at the waiter.

Say, "Yuck!" if you don't like something.

HOW TO SERVE LIKE A WIMBLEDON CHAMPION

Keep calm and take the time to get into position. At all times, remember: balance, timing, and rhythm.

1. Grip the racket, spreading your fingers around the handle without squeezing too hard. Keep your arm relaxed. Take the ball in the other hand.

2. Facing the net, point your racket to where you want the ball to go and use your throwing hand (this will be your left hand if you are right-handed) to support the ball lightly.

3. Raise your hands together just a short way, then bring them down together. As you do this, start to turn your body so that you are sideways to the court. At the same time, transfer your weight from your front foot to your back foot. Try to keep this sequence of movements smooth and coordinated.

4. Raise your throwing arm (left if you're playing right-handed) into an upright

position to release the ball above your head. A good height to throw the ball is about 6 inches above your normal reach. Keep your arm straight to help throw the ball accurately and make sure you don't release the ball too soon — it will fly at an angle toward the net and force you to lean forward to hit it.

5. While the ball is in the air, you need to bring the racket fluidly back and up, ready to hit the ball. This is the most difficult part of the action, because at the same time as coordinating your arms you also need to transfer your weight from your back foot to your front.

6. As the ball gets to the top of the throw, direct the racket at the ball in a swift throwing action. Aim to hit the ball at full stretch, with your racket arm straight, at the highest point you can reach it. The higher you make contact, the more power you can generate, and the harder and faster the ball will go.

7. Follow the motion through with your body, then look to recover quickly, ready for your next shot.

HOW TO GET RID OF HICCUPS

Swallow a teaspoon of sugar,

or gulp down a glass of water,

or eat a piece of dry bread slowly,

or gargle water,

or drink water from the farthest side of the glass rim,

or hold your breath and count backward,

or try all of these at once — you'll probably feel so ill and confused that you'll forget about your hiccups.

HOW TO MUMMIFY AN ANCIENT EGYPTIAN

You are an ancient Egyptian, working as an embalmer. The family of a rich noblewoman who has recently died comes to you. They wish to preserve her body to make sure her soul has somewhere to reside during the afterlife.

1. First, using special custom-made hooks and spoons, you draw out the brain through the nose. This is very tricky, as you have to be careful not to damage the face.

2. You then take out the internal organs (the lungs, liver, stomach, intestines, and so on) through a cut made in the left side of the tummy. The heart, however, you leave where it is.

3. Your helpers then wash the body in spiced palm wine.

4. When that's done, you cover the body, packing it inside as well as out (especially all around the heart), with natron, a mineral salt found in dried lake beds. You leave the natron there for 40 days to absorb all the moisture from the body. In the meantime, you have been treating the removed organs in the same way. These used to be stored in special canopic jars and buried alongside the mummy;

you, however, use the new practice of preserving them, wrapping them up and popping them back into the body.

5. After 40 days, the body should be completely dried out, and look shriveled and wrinkled. You clean away the natron and rub oils into the skin to soften it. You pad out the body with strong-smelling herbs and spices, mud, sawdust, rags, and other bits of linen to stop it from sinking in and losing its shape. That done, you pop out the eyes and replace them with false ones.

6. Wrapping the body can take many days, as there are 20 layers of linen strips — hundreds of yards — to wind around the body. As you wind the bandages around the mummy, you slip in various charms, made of precious metals and precious stones, among the linen strips. On some of the bandages you write prayers and magic words. You use resin glue to keep the bandages in place.

7. As your current customer is from a noble family, you have been asked to place a gold-leafed mask over the almost fully bandaged head. (You made sure that the mask-maker managed a reasonable likeness of the dead noblewoman before you bound up the head.) Now you notice with approval that he has made her eyes bigger and nose smaller than they were in life — she might as well be more beautiful in the afterlife than she was in the life she has just left.

8. Your job is done, and you hand the mummy over to the specialist craftsmen who have been working on her coffin and tomb.

HOW TO RIP A PHONE BOOK IN HALF

1. With the spine of the book toward you, place your hands on top of the book and grip it with your little and ring fingers. Bend the book into a U shape by pushing with your thumbs.

2. Now hold the book tightly with all your fingers and, while keeping the U shape in place, bend the book the other way so that the pages form a V shape.

3. As you continue to bend the edges of the book down, the pages will start to split.

4. Push with one of your hands and pull with the other to rip the book in half.

HOW TO RACE STICK BOATS

1. Find at least one other person to compete against.

2. Collect some sticks of all shapes and sizes.

3. Find a small footbridge over a stream.

4. Select a stick and compare it with those belonging to the other competitors to make sure you can tell them apart.

5. Stand side by side on the bridge, facing upstream.

6. Secretly check for fast-moving currents or slow, reedy areas and trapped logs.

7. On the count of three, drop your sticks into the water.

8. Quickly cross to the downstream side of the bridge and watch for the sticks to emerge.

9. The owner of the first stick to float out from under the bridge is the winner.

HOW TO SEE THROUGH YOUR HAND

1. Take a cardboard tube (from a roll of paper towels or toilet paper) and look through it with your right eye.

2. Place the edge of your left hand over the end of the tube with the palm facing you.

3. With both eyes open, stare at the point where the tube and the edge of your hand meet and you'll see that you have a hole in your hand.

HOW TO WRITE A QUICK POEM

A homework topic that usually provokes groans starts with the words, "Write a poem about . . ." If the topic is boring, it's even harder to be creative, but here is a quick, unfailing way to impress your teachers and be the envy of friends.

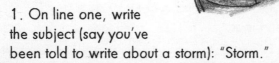

1. On line one, write the subject (say you've been told to write about a storm): "Storm."

2. On line two, write down two descriptive words that spring to your mind when you think of storms: "Dark, angry."

3. On line three, write three verbs (action words) connected to a storm: "Blows, howls, crashes."

4. On line four, write a thought that comes to you: "Will it never end."

5. On line five, write another phrase to describe the subject (i.e., storm): "Nature's rage."

6. Storm.

   Dark, angry,

   Blows, howls, crashes.

   Will it never end,

   Nature's rage?

OR: Me.

   Modest but wonderful,

   I can, I know, and I do.

   The best at everything,

   That's me!

You will soon do much better than this. And then, if you like, you can refine your new skill — make it rhyme or add more lines as you want. Soon your friends will be coming to you for help writing messages in greeting cards.

HOW TO GET OUT OF QUICKSAND

Whatever you do, don't think of all those films in which a character is gradually sucked, struggling and screaming, into the depths of the quicksand, then vanishes from sight with a faint plop. Remind yourself instead that you can float on quicksand — it is, in fact, a lot easier to float in quicksand than in water.

1. The worst thing to do is to thrash around and move your arms and legs through the mixture — you will only succeed in forcing yourself farther down into the quicksand.

2. If you are heading to an area where you think there may be quicksand, including riverbanks, beaches, and marshes, carry a stout stick. If you find yourself sinking in quicksand, lay the stick down on the surface of the quicksand and gently slide onto it on your back. Your body weight will spread out across the stick and you will find it easier to float. If you don't have a stick, turn onto your back and slowly spread out your arms and legs to increase your surface area.

3. Once afloat, move very slowly and carefully using your arms, and edge your way toward firm ground.

HOW TO MAKE A SIMPLE RAFT

You will need: four straight wooden poles, about 6 feet long and 3 to 4 inches thick; three shorter wooden poles of the same thickness, but about 4 feet long; at least 200 feet of $\frac{3}{16}$ of an inch–thick nylon cord; at least 12 strong 1.3-gallon empty rectangular plastic containers of the kind used for laundry detergent (caps should be screwed on tightly); any planks or boards, at least 6 feet long, that you can find; nails, a hammer, a screwdriver, and scissors.

1. Lay the end of one of the shorter poles over the end of a longer one and at right angles to it, and lash them together with the nylon cord. Lay the other end of the shorter pole over the end of a second longer one, and lash together; then lash the free ends of the two longer poles under each end of a second shorter one — creating a rectangular structure.

2. Lash each end of the third shorter pole across and over the middle of the two longer ones; then lash the third and fourth long poles beneath the middle of the three shorter crossways poles — the distance between these two long poles should be just wider than the narrowest side of one of the empty containers. You should now have a rectangle consisting of four long poles crossed by three shorter ones laid on top of them.

3. Now lash three of the empty containers at even intervals along the outside of one of the outer long poles, the caps pointing toward the stern (rear) of the raft. Repeat along the outside of the other outer long pole, and then again between the two center long poles.

4. Launch the raft in shallow water and ask an adult to test its buoyancy — ideally, the level of the deck should be about 6 inches above the surface of the water when a person is sitting on the raft. If necessary, lash more containers to the long poles (you can get six containers along each pole) until you achieve the right degree of buoyancy. But remember that as you add more weight when you fix the decking, the raft will sit lower in the water.

5. Now fix your decking of boards or planks to the three shorter cross poles — lash them in place, or otherwise nail or screw them to the cross poles. There can be gaps between the deck planks — in fact, the lighter you build your raft, the better it will float. The decking planks don't need to touch one another.

6. Relaunch the raft and climb aboard.

A useful knot for putting together a raft is the square lashing. Find out how to do it in a knot book or on the Internet.

HOW TO TEACH A PARAKEET TO TALK

To ensure you have a bird with the ability to talk, and one that you can train, choose a young male Australian parakeet, or an English, Ringnecked, Alexandrine, or Plumheaded parakeet.

Parakeets develop their communication skills by talking to one another, so if you can, keep two or three birds. If not, a useful trick is to put a mirror in your bird's cage. This will cheer him up and he will chat happily with his own reflection just as if it were another bird in the cage. Be sure to remove the mirror when you start teaching the parakeet to talk — or he may prefer to talk to himself.

To train your bird, first you must make friends with him — spend time with him, talk to him, keep his cage clean, give him plenty of clean water, and make sure he is well fed. Train him to sit on your hand or finger.

To teach him to talk, speak clearly and slowly, repeating the word or phrase over and over. Parakeets tend to speed up words when they repeat them, so speak slowly and your parakeet will pronounce the word correctly.

Parakeets can recognize and pick up certain sounds better than others.

They are best with consonants such as d, k, t, p, or b. A traditional phrase, such as "Hello, how are you?", isn't very good to start with, since it is hard for the bird to say.

It is important to speak to your parakeet regularly and to speak to him for more than a few minutes — if possible, train him at least half an hour a day.

During lessons, cover the top and three sides of his cage with a towel or cloth, so that he is not distracted by anything.

Don't move on to a second word or phrase until he can repeat the first one. Be patient; once he has learned a few words, it will take much less time to learn more.

Once a parakeet learns to repeat words, you can teach him to recognize an object and say its name, like a book or pen. Simply hold the object up to the bird and repeat the word.

After a while you can train your bird to recognize you by your name (or whatever you choose to call yourself). "Good morning, Boss," your bird might greet you. But be careful not to refer to any of your family members by nicknames you would prefer to keep secret. Your new talkative pet might give you away!

HOW TO HOOT WITH YOUR HANDS

1. Use your hands to form a cave with only one entrance, the slit between your thumbs. There are two ways for you to make this cave:

a) Clasp your hands together with the fingers of one hand (A) folded over the other between the thumb and index finger, and the fingers of the other hand (B) folded over the outside of hand A. Hand A's thumb rests lightly on hand B's. Now adjust your hands to form a cave between them, with the two outer edges of your hands right against each other. Make sure there are no gaps between the edges of your hands or any of your fingers, and make sure that the wrist edges of your hands are pressed together.

b) Instead of clasping your hands together, lace your fingers tightly together so there are no gaps for air to get through. Make sure the wrist edges of your hands are pressed tightly and then pull your palms away from each other, so as to form your cave.

2. For either kind of cave, relax your thumbs so that they are slightly bent, with the side of the nails touching. Line up the upper part of your thumbs with the underside of your index finger. You will now have a slit — wider in the middle than the top or bottom — between your thumbs.

3. Place your lips on your thumb knuckles, the upper lip resting on the bases of your thumbnails and the bottom lip resting just below your knuckles. Be very careful not to close the air hole with your lower lip.

4. Blow steadily — and not too hard — through your knuckles. If you're lucky you'll hear a raspy almost-hoot (if you're very lucky you might hear a kind of whistly hoot); if you're not so lucky you'll just hear a puffing sound.

Adjust your fingers and thumbs carefully, make sure your cave is still sealed tight, and that the air you are blowing through the top of the air hole is coming out through the bottom (you can probably feel it coming out). It can help to have damp, even wet, hands.

5. Keep trying. Sooner or later you will get a good hoot and, as you practice, it will become easier and the sound will become clearer. Then you can start experimenting with blowing harder or softer, bending and flexing your fingers and thumbs, squeezing your hands together, etc., to change the note.

HOW TO SPEAK IN CODE

Eggy-peggy: Add "egg" before each vowel.
Example: "Eggi eggam thegge beggest." ("I am the best.")

Gree: Add "gree" to the end of every word.
Example: "Igree amgree thegree bestgree."

Na: Add "na" to the end of every word.
Example: "Ina amna thena bestna."

Pig Latin: Move the first letter to the end of the word and add "ay" to it.
Example: "Iay maay hetay estbay."

HOW TO MAKE A BALLOON DOG

1. Blow up a long, skinny balloon, leaving 1 ¼ inches of unblown balloon at the end.

2. Tie a knot at the end of the balloon.

3. Make a twist in the balloon about 2 inches from the knotted end.

4. Make two more twists about 1 inch apart from each other, after the first twist. Make sure not to let go of the balloon.

5. Twist the two smaller bubbles together. These will become the ears. You will see that you have already made the dog's head.

6. Make three more twists about 2 inches apart and twist these sections together. These will be the neck and the two front legs.

7. Now make three more twists: one for the dog's body, and two more about 2 inches apart for its back legs.

8. Fold and twist the two smaller sections together and twist the legs down. Use a felt-tip pen to draw on eyes and a mouth, if you like.

Warning: Ask an adult for help when making your balloon dog. Be sure small children and pets do not chew on whole or partial balloons.

HOW TO BUILD A CAMPFIRE

You never know when you will need to stay warm in the great outdoors and it is essential to know how to make a safe, successful campfire. For this activity, ask an adult to help you.

1. Make sure you have the permission of the person who owns the land. Choose a suitable spot — away from anything that might catch fire, especially trees, bushes, and buildings. Make sure that your belongings are out of the way and remove stones from the area, as these can get very hot and explode. It is a good idea to have a bucket of water or sand (or soil) close by in case your fire gets too enthusiastic.

2. If the site for the fire is grassy, cut around and under a 3 foot square of grass. Lift it out, lay it right side up, and sprinkle it with water. The grass should stay fresh until you replace it after you have broken camp. Make your fire in the space from which you lifted the grass.

3. You will need three kinds of burnable material: tinder, kindling, and fuel. Tinder is light stuff that catches fire easily — like shredded bark, dry grass, or dry pine needles. Gather enough to half fill a standard-size bucket. Kindling is slim, dry twigs — no thicker than a pencil. Collect at least enough to fill the same bucket.

4. For fuel you will need firewood — dead, dry sticks thicker than kindling. Start by filling your bucket — you can collect more fuel as necessary. Make sure your fuel is neither green nor wet, as this will make the fire smoke.

5. Pile up the tinder, then lean the kindling over it to build a triangular structure like a tepee; over this, place some of the firewood, also standing and leaning in. Too much fuel will smother your fire — there should be plenty of air space beneath the kindling and fuel.

6. Light the tinder. If it takes, the kindling will catch fire, too, and as it burns more strongly, the firewood should take.

7. You will soon have a merry little fire. But keep an eye on it — fire is sneaky. And when you have finished, make sure you put the fire out completely — not a single glowing ember should be left. Spread the ashes out, and pour some water on them to be on the safe side. Replace the grass you removed.

HOW TO TIE A TIE

Lift up your shirt collar and put the tie around your neck so that both ends hang down in front. The wide end should hang about 1 foot lower than the thin end. Put your collar back down.

1. Cross the wide end over the thin end near the collar, then take it around underneath the thin end.

2. Bring the wide end over the thin end again and back underneath. Push it up through the back of the V shape made by the partially formed knot.

3. Bring the wide end forward (i.e., away from you) through the V and down through the front loop of the knot.

4. Hold the thin end and slide the knot up to your neck. Hold the knot and, with the other hand, pull on each end of the tie until the knot is tight (but not too tight!).

HOW TO ANNOY YOUR BROTHERS AND SISTERS

With these tricks, your brothers and sisters will be so annoyed they won't even want to be in the same room as you! But beware of the consequences — don't do any of these things unless you're prepared for war.

Hang around when your brother or sister is lounging in front of the TV and, when you hear your parents approaching, quickly start straightening up the room — you'll get endless praise from your parents, while your sibling will be frowned upon for his or her laziness. To keep yourself amused while you wait for your parents to see you working so hard, find as many excuses as possible for walking slowly past the TV screen and blocking your brother's or sister's view.

Tie a knot in one of your brother's pajama legs. Do it on random nights so he never expects it. When he puts them on, he will probably fall over with a thud.

If your brother or sister has a girlfriend or boyfriend, it's just too good an opportunity to miss: leave humiliating photos of him or her lying around throughout the house; bring up the subject of your many farting competitions over dinner; if there's an extra phone, make burping sounds on the line when they talk to each other.

When your brother or sister is about to go out, make sure that whatever is most vital to him or her is missing. After ten minutes of furious searching, you will "find" it. The first time you might be met with thanks, but your brother or sister will soon catch on and get very annoyed.

Get a *TV Guide* and look up what is on at the same time as your sister's favorite shows, then tell your parents that you need to watch something on the other channel for school. Act totally bored by the program whenever your parents are out of sight.

When you do homework together, claim to need everything that he or she is using — the calculator, the ruler, etc. While you wait to "use" these items, drum on the table, or hum to yourself. When they finally give up the item, find something pointless to do with it — use the calculator to write the word *shell* upside down (77345), and the ruler to underline your name on your notebook.

HOW TO TAKE A PENALTY KICK

You have three things to consider: the goalkeeper, how you kick the ball, and where you send the ball.

1. **Goalkeeper:** The goalie's aim is to distract you and put you off your kick. Check the goalie's position but don't pay him any other attention. If you look at the goalie, he's gained an advantage.

The goalie's second aim is to save the penalty, either by predicting which way you'll kick the ball or by waiting, following, and stopping the ball.

2. **Ball:** There are two favored techniques for kicking the ball. One is to kick the ball hard with the laces of your shoe — the advantage is that it's a powerful shot; the disadvantage is that there is more risk of the ball going wide or straight over the crossbar. The second technique is to kick the ball with the side of the foot, with less power but more accuracy.

3. **Aim:** Before kicking, select the spot where you wish to direct the ball, but do not look at this position and risk giving it away to the goalie. You might want to try tricking the goalie by approaching the ball as if you're going to kick it in one direction, but then kick it the other way; or by running up to the ball as though you are about to hit it hard with the laces of your shoe, but instead use the side of your foot to place the ball to the right or the left. The best odds are to aim high and preferably to the left or right, as a low center shot stands less chance of getting past the goalie.

HOW TO HYPNOTIZE A CHICKEN

This will work on any chicken, but if you know any particularly laid-back, chilled-out birds, they'd probably be good to practice on. Lulling a chicken into a stupor won't cause it any harm—handle the chicken firmly and confidently, but remember to be very gentle with it.

1. Lay the chicken down on its side, with one wing tucked under its body, and its head flat on the floor.

2. Use your left hand to gently hold the chicken steady and say reassuring things such as, "Don't worry, I'm a vegetarian," in a calm voice.

3. With the index finger of your right hand trace a line, 1 foot long, straight out from the tip of its beak. Repeat this movement until the chicken is in a hypnotic trance, and everyone watching is impressed by your incredible talent.

4. To wake your chicken, gradually raise your voice until it comes to and runs away.

HOW TO TREAT STINGS

You can recognize if a person is allergic to a sting if they have difficulty breathing, their pulse speeds up, they collapse, or areas of the body away from the site of the sting swell up. If you see any of these signs, be sure to immediately call an ambulance, but also ask the person if they've got treatment with them (some carry an adrenaline shot ready to be injected). Likewise, if they've been very badly stung or have been stung in the mouth or eyes, call an ambulance at once.

Otherwise, when a person is stung, they will suffer only short-lived pain and some discomfort that can be soothed by pressing something cool on the affected area or rubbing it with an ice cube.

Bee stings: Quickly scrape out the stinger using your fingernail. Wash the site with soap and water. Apply a compress of ice wrapped in a washcloth (10 minutes on, 10 minutes off). To relieve any itching, apply calamine lotion or a mixture of baking soda and water.

Jellyfish stings: If you are stung by a box jellyfish or a Portuguese man-of-war, seek medical attention immediately. For other jellyfish stings, soak or rinse the area in vinegar to help relieve the pain.

Nettle stings: Rubbing with dock leaves (a green-leaved weed with clusters of small greenish or reddish petal-less flowers) provides the best relief. If you can't find dock leaves, try mint (recognizable by its scent).

HOW TO CLIMB A PALM TREE

You need to be barefoot to get a grip on the tree, but wear a long-sleeved shirt and pants to protect yourself from a bad scraping. Palm trees can be dangerous to climb, as they can reach heights of up to 80 feet. Don't attempt a climb unless an adult is present.

Climb like a frog. Flex your legs on each side of the tree with the soles of your feet firmly against the sides of the trunk. Your legs should look like those of a frog, bent knees sticking out on either side of you. Move one hand up, against the other side of the trunk, and place the other hand at chest level on your side of the tree. Move yourself up by straightening your legs, shifting your weight to your hands, and, with a jumplike motion, bringing up both of your feet at the same time to return to the frog position, progressing up the tree as you do so. Rest after every few "jumps." When you can reach the palm leaves, grab hold and make your way up to the coconuts.

Going down. Either return to the froglike position, feet first, and jump down step by step, or lower your hands one by one behind the trunk while allowing the soles of your feet to slide down against the trunk.

HOW TO BE FIRST OFF THE STARTING BLOCK

1. As you wait for the starter's commands, breathe gently and try to relax — to help your body run efficiently and quickly.

2. **"On your mark."** Crouch on one knee and place your hands just behind the starting line, forming a high bridge between your fingers and thumbs. Your hands should be placed slightly farther apart than your shoulders. Keep your eyes fixed on the ground ahead of you to help your balance, focus, and relaxation. Try not to allow anything to distract you.

3. **"Get set."** Raise your hips so they're just higher than your shoulders. Keep your head at a comfortable angle — don't try to look up at the track but don't look right down, either. Lean your body as far forward as you can and aim to begin running without stumbling. Breathe in. Be ready for the starting signal.

4. **"Go."** Breathe out hard and pump your arms and legs. To start with, try not to take too-big strides; wait until you're balanced and running rhythmically. Thrust your elbows as high as possible with each backward swing and drive your legs with a high knee action.

5. Keep going, and leave everyone else behind.

HOW TO PLAY A TRICK ON
THE WHOLE CLASS

Before you play your trick, enlist a partner in crime, explain how the trick works, and prepare a key word to use that only the two of you know about.

1. Announce to your class that you have telepathic powers. To prove your point, you will leave the room while the class, or a single volunteer, chooses an object from the room and tells your partner what it is.

2. When you return, your partner will ask you what object the volunteer is thinking of — "Could it be the lamp?," "Is it the window?," "Or is it the green plant?" Consider each of these questions, as though connecting with your powers, but to each one answer, "No."

3. Then your partner asks, "Is it the red chair?" You answer, "No," but they have alerted you with the word "red." This is the key word that you have chosen, and when your partner uses this key word you know that the next question they ask will be the right answer. "Is it the picture on the wall?" your partner asks next, to which you reply, "Yes." "It was?" gasps the astonished class. And you take your bow.

4. Pick five or six key words and alternate between them ("red," "big," "on the table," etc.). Or use signals such as the way your partner points or the way you enter the room — putting three fingers around the edge of the door could signal to your partner to say the correct object on his third question. Your class will never be able to spot how the trick works and your answers will always be correct.

HOW TO WRITE A SECRET MESSAGE

All top secrets are best kept and passed in code. Devising your own code to use with a friend is the best way of ensuring no one will crack it.

1. Break your message into groups of two letters:

> I AM THE BEST AT EVERYTHING
> IA MT HE BE ST AT EV ER YT HI NG

2. Then reverse the letters in each pair:

> AI TM EH EB TS TA VE RE TY IH GN

3. Now run the letters together:

> AITMEHEBTSTAVERETYIHGN

Think about how you could adapt this code: adding a dummy letter between each pair of letters, swapping adjacent pairs, or reversing every other pair.

HOW TO READ A COMPASS

orienting mark   compass needle

direction-of-travel line

compass housing
(which can be turned)

base plate   compass dial

1. Hold the compass flat in front of you so as to allow the compass needle to float freely. Assuming there is nothing magnetic close by, the needle will point to magnetic north. (Make sure there's nothing magnetic around, though — if, for instance, you had a magnet in your pocket the needle would point to that instead of to the north. Large metal objects — an iron gate, for instance — can also affect magnetic compasses.)

2. Rotate the compass housing until the orienting mark — N (for north) or the 0° symbol — lines up with the needle, making sure that it is the north end of the needle (indicated by a distinguishing mark — say by its being red) and not the south end hovering above the N or 0° mark.

3. Now you know where the magnetic north lies, which means that you now also know where south, east, west, and all the other compass points are.

4. To use the compass to find your way to, say, a distant hill, aim the base plate of the compass so that the direction-of-travel line points exactly at the hill.

5. Turn the compass housing until the orienting mark is beneath the north end of the compass needle, then double-check to make sure that the direction-of-travel line is still pointing at the hill. You now have your bearings — and if you have taken them accurately, by following the direction-of-travel line while keeping the compass needle over the orienting mark, you will reach the hill.

HOW TO FALL WITHOUT HURTING YOURSELF ... MUCH

1. Try to relax and not fight the fall — unless it is clear that falling would lead to serious injury (e.g., if there are unfriendly hazards like rocks or heavy machinery), in which case, try to send your body the other way.

2. Try not to land hands down, as you could injure your wrists, elbows, or shoulders.

3. Attempt to fall on your side rather than your front or back. Half-turn or roll, if necessary, to land on the fleshier parts of your body.

4. Don't allow your body to open out. Tuck up instead — your chin firmly against your chest, arms bent at the elbows to protect your head and face.

5. If you're on a bicycle, let go of it, try to swing your leg from under the bike, and push the bike away from you. Always wear a helmet to protect your head if you should fall.

HOW TO POP A WHEELIE

Impress your friends with this amazing bit of stunt riding. A wheelie is difficult to perform on a road bike. It is easier on a BMX-style bike because of the lower center of gravity. Ask an adult to spot you as you practice this tricky stunt.

1. Sit on a bike.

2. Start pedaling until you're going about 5 miles per hour.

3. Stand on the pedals.

4. Lean back over the rear wheel.

5. Pull sharply on the handlebar while still pedaling.

6. As the front wheel rises, balance your weight and your pedaling to maintain the wheelie.

Tip: Keep your wheel at a good height and be careful not to flip over onto your back — using the back brake will help prevent this.

HOW TO TAKE THE BEST PHOTOS

1. The most interesting photos capture a moment that might never happen again. As such moments can rarely be planned, try to keep your camera within easy reach.

2. When taking a photo of a person or animal, try to get a feeling of life and immediacy by establishing eye contact — or rather, eye to lens contact.

3. Manual focusing can produce excellent results but quite often things change while you're still fiddling and the moment is lost. Automatic focusing is quicker but will assume that the object in the middle of the frame is what you wish to have in focus — what's behind, in front, and to the sides will not come out as sharply. You might be able to lock the focus. To do this: You first center the subject of your picture in the frame and then press and hold the shutter button halfway down. Then, still holding the shutter halfway down, you change the position of your camera so the subject is framed how you want it to be. Then press the shutter button to take the picture.

4. Some cameras have an automatic flash — this can be annoying if you are trying for an artistic shot using low-level lighting. Again, it might be possible to override the automatic flash. With many, though, the flash is manual — so remember to set it when it is needed.

Avoid taking photos too close up with a flash, as the subject will appear bleached. The other common flash problem is "red eye," in which the light is reflected off the back of the subject's eye. Some cameras have a red-eye reduction feature (with two flashes, the first to make the pupils smaller, the second to light up the subject). If yours does not, you could try flashing a bright light in your subject's face just before pressing the shutter (warn them first, though).

5. Visualize your photos as a whole. Look at the surrounding area — rather than just your subject. Choose your location carefully, check the background, and remove or add items if necessary. Adjust lighting (there might be bright sun pouring through the window straight into your lens, or too little light).

6. Note that the morning or evening sun gives the most attractive light — in the middle of the day it can be too glaring. If you are taking a photograph in sunshine, be sure that the sun does not fall upon your lens. You might find that sunlight takes color and definition from a subject's face — or exaggerates certain features.

7. With landscapes, lighting is perhaps even more important than the location — in soft dawn light a view of a river curving through a field is beautiful, in the noonday sun it is flat and glaring, and in the light of a sunset it is dramatic.

8. Experiment with taking photos from different angles. You do not have to be standing at eye level — kneel down, or climb up on something to find the best perspective.

9. As always, practice is the key. For this reason a digital camera is probably the best, as you can see and keep or delete your photos instantly.

HOW TO TIE A KNOT WITHOUT LETTING GO OF THE ENDS

1. Lay the piece of string in front of you and cross your arms so that one hand is over the other arm and one hand is under.

2. Keeping your arms folded, pick up each end of the string.

3. Keeping hold of the two ends, uncross your arms.

4. Ta-da! The string is tied in a knot.

HOW TO SURVIVE A VOLCANIC ERUPTION

First of all, know what you are up against. Deep below the surface of the earth, a buildup of gases and the movement of the crustal plates increase pressure to a point where it can no longer be contained. The result is an explosion of boiling magma (molten rock) in the form of lava, flaming gases, and red-hot fragments of rock and dust. Pretty scary stuff.

At any given time there are usually at least 12 volcanoes erupting somewhere in the world. If you find yourself living near one, make sure you are prepared.

Stock up on provisions of bottled water, food, medical supplies, blankets, warm clothing, a battery-powered radio, and batteries in case power lines are cut. Collect water in your bathtub, sinks, and containers as water supplies may quickly become polluted.

In the event of an eruption, seek shelter at home and don't leave unless advised to by the authorities. Keep listening to the radio or TV for news and advice.

If you go outside, wear a mask and goggles to keep volcanic ash out of your eyes and lungs. Keep gutters and roofs clear of settling ash, which could bring the house down upon you.

If possible, stay indoors and stay with an adult.

If you are caught outside during an eruption, be aware of the hazards that come with an eruption: flying debris, hot gases, lava flows, explosions, mudslides, avalanches, boiling water spray from geysers, and floods. If you are in an area that could experience a lava flow, never try to cross it.

Look for hills and head toward them. They may afford you some protection from the destructive and devastating effects of the eruption.

HOW TO JUGGLE

Take one ball and throw it from hand to hand. Make sure each throw goes straight up and to the same height (about eye level). Catch the ball at waist level.

Now move on to two balls, one in each hand. Throw the first ball, A, as described above. Wait until it is about to descend and then throw the second ball, B, up underneath the first. If you can't react quickly enough at first, try throwing the balls higher to give yourself more time to catch them. If you find the balls are going forward, throw them slightly in, toward yourself. Continue practicing with the two balls until you feel confident. Then practice starting with your second hand.

Repeat these moves, throwing the balls higher as you grow more confident. Always have at least one ball in the air, and never more than one in either hand. Watch the balls as they reach their highest point and don't reach up to them; let them come down to you.

Now try juggling with three balls. Here's how:

1. In your left hand hold ball A between your thumb, first, and middle fingers, and ball C between your ring finger, pinky, and your thumb. Ball B is in your right hand.

2. Throw ball A up; when it reaches its highest point, throw ball B. Catch ball A in your right hand.

3. When ball B reaches its highest point, throw ball C. Catch ball B in your left hand.

4. When ball C is at its highest point, throw ball A. Catch ball C. Throw ball B up, and so on.

HOW TO READ SOMEONE'S MIND

Ask a friend to pick a number between 1 and 5. Ask them to multiply that number by 9. Ask them to add the digits of the number they get. Now ask them to subtract 5 from their answer.

Tell your friend to think of the letter in the alphabet that corresponds to their number (1 is A, 2 is B, and so on). Tell them to think of a country in Europe that starts with that letter. Now ask them to think of an animal that starts with the last letter of that country. And then a color that starts with the last letter of their animal. Now tell them that you know what they are thinking, and that it is an orange kangaroo in Denmark. Chances are that you're right.

HOW TO SAVE THE WORLD

1. Walk or bike to school instead of being driven.

2. Save electricity by switching off appliances when you are not using them.

3. Recycle everything you can — either by reusing items for other purposes or by taking them to recycling centers.

4. Take an interest in environmental issues: on television, in newspapers, and on the Internet.

5. Bring reusable bags when shopping, and refuse new ones when offered.

6. Take quick showers instead of deep baths.

7. Use energy-efficient lightbulbs.

HOW TO MAKE A SQUEALER

The high-pitched squeal that some young animals make when in need will attract their mother as well as predators and other merely curious animals. You can make a device that imitates this squeal out of a hazel twig. Use it to see what animals you can attract.

You will need: one straight length of dry twig about 1 inch thick and 6 inches long, a pocketknife with a strong, sharp blade, three strong rubber bands — one of which must be approximately 3½ inches long and $3/16$ of an inch wide unstretched.

1. Trim the ends of the twig and cut off any minor twiglets and bumps.

2. Ask an adult to help you with this part. With the knife (careful of your fingers), split the twig lengthwise into halves. To do this, stand the twig on one end and rest the blade of the knife across the other end so as to bisect it. Press down on the knife blade until it has started to cut. Then, holding the knife handle, tap the end of the blade repeatedly with a piece of wood to move it down through the twig.

3. Take one half of the twig and mark its center. Then with the knife, cut across the width of the twig half at two points, each about ¾ of an inch from the marked center,

to a depth of about $\frac{1}{16}$ of an inch. Using the knife, carefully scrape out the wood between the two cuts. You should now have one half of the twig with a shallow dip, 1 ½ inches long, across its center.

4. Repeat with the other half of the twig, making sure that the two ends of each half-twig match, so that they will fit together again.

5. Take the longer rubber band and stretch it lengthwise along one half of the twig, so that it lies flat and runs over the center of the dip in the middle. Then place the two halves of the twig back together, trapping the long rubber band running between them.

6. Bind each end of the twig with one of the other shorter rubber bands, making as many turns as necessary to keep the twig halves firmly together.

7. Hold the twig across your mouth with your lips over the dip in the center. Blow gently. Provided the rubber band trapped in the dip is tight enough, the effect should be a loud high-pitched squealing sound caused by the air passing over the stretched rubber band. You can experiment with variations of the note by adjusting the tension of the long rubber band: tighter = higher pitched; looser = lower pitched.

8. Blow for about two to four seconds; the harder you blow, the louder and, to a limited extent, the higher the pitch; ending the call with a short hard blast will produce a high-pitched squeal, as though a young animal was in immediate danger.

9. Conceal yourself in a hedge, ditch, etc. Blow your squealer. In this way, depending on where you are, you might attract deer, rabbits, skunks, raccoons, local cats and dogs — as well as curious or annoyed neighbors.

HOW TO REPAIR A FLAT TIRE

1. You'll need a puncture-repair kit, the bike manual, and any necessary tools. Check the tire for obvious causes of the flat — e.g., a nail or piece of glass. Unscrew the valve to let any remaining air out of the tube. Remove the tire from the wheel carefully so as not to pinch the tube. Pull the tube out, pressing the valve through the hole in the rim (if it is secured with a rim nut, unscrew that first).

2. Look for the puncture. If it is not obvious, replace the valve, pump the tube up a little, and listen for the hiss of escaping air, or dunk it in water. A stream of bubbles will reveal the site of the puncture.

3. Once you've found the puncture, draw a circle around it. Making sure that the tube is completely dry, lightly roughen the area around the puncture with fine sandpaper. This will allow the glue to bond better — don't be tempted to skip this step.

4. Apply a thin coat of rubber solution over the area where the leak is, covering an area slightly larger than the patch. Allow it to dry completely — three to five minutes (be patient) — if you don't, the patch will probably come off.

5. Take a patch of the right size and put a tiny blob of solution on its contact surface, then at once wipe off with your finger all but a very thin coat. Wait another three to five minutes. Then apply the patch, with the center over the puncture, in one try (don't try to pull it off and reposition it), smoothing it down to get rid of any air bubbles. Press firmly.

6. Keep pressing it down really hard for at least a minute, especially around the edges. Wait for a couple of minutes and then carefully peel the backing paper or plastic off the patch. If an edge of the patch lifts with it, quickly press it back down; then try lifting the backing again from the other side. If the whole patch comes away with the backing, you'll have to start again with a new patch. (Self-adhesive patches do exist — but they do not always work very well.)

7. Once you've removed the backing, press down on the patch to seal the edges — then it's time to replace the inner tube. Dust it with French chalk (from your puncture-repair kit — grate it on your sandpaper), especially all around the patch so it doesn't stick to the inside of the tire. That done, replace the valve and pump a little air into the tube; this makes it easier to replace.

8. As you replace the tube, make sure the valve stem is correctly positioned and that the tube is not pinched or creased. If everything looks okay, then pump the tire up to normal pressure. You've done it — but keep an eye on the tire for a while.

HOW TO MAKE A TUMBLER

With just a gentle push, send a folded piece of paper tumbling! Here's how:

1. Fold an 8½ x 11 inch piece of paper in half lengthwise, then unfold it to leave a crease. Fold, then unfold a triangle as shown.

2. Fold the top of the paper over from dot A to dot B as shown.

3. Again, fold over the top from dot C to dot D as shown.

4. Fold in the top corners to make two right-angled triangles.

5. Fold the top over from dot E to dot F.

6. Fold the two edges into the center crease, then unfold.

7. Fold in the two bottom corners diagonally to the creases you just made.

8. Fold the bottom
edge up to the top
of the triangles.

9. Fold up two edges
along the original creases
so they stand upright.

10. Place your tumbler on a flat surface with the thick edge
up. Gently push the top edge, then sit back and watch it
tumble.

HOW TO TELL IF A PERSON IS LYING

As the person is telling you his or her version of events, keep your ears and eyes open for telltale signs.

1. Unusual stuttering or stammering may suggest that they are nervous and could be an indication that the person is lying.

2. Note any changes in the person's pattern of speech. See if they seem high pitched, put on a silly voice, speak too quickly or slowly, or use unusual words. For instance, does it sound as though the person has memorized their story by heart?

3. Watch out for visible signs of stress or nervousness — sweating, twitching, scratching, rubbing, looking away, shifting around, crossing and uncrossing the legs, rapid breathing — all of these indicate that the person might not be telling the whole truth.

4. There are other signs to consider. Get the person to go over the story again — but not in sequence. Ask probing questions. Does he or she seem confused? Or appear to contradict him- or herself? Ask about unimportant details (along the lines of "What color was his T-shirt?"). Someone who is telling the truth is less likely to get muddled and anxious, even though they might have forgotten some of the details.

5. Some say that if the "suspect," when questioned, looks to the left, they are inventing and if they look to the right, they are remembering. Perhaps you could put this theory to the test.

HOW TO DO A CARTWHEEL

To perform a well-executed cartwheel, you have to be quick and approach the turn with energy and confidence.

1. Stand with your right leg in front, knees bent slightly, and arms up straight.

2. Reach forward and down with your right arm, throwing your left leg up as you do so.

3. Your left arm will follow very quickly, and as, or just before, it touches the ground, kick your right leg up in the air, also. For a brief moment you are in a handstand.

4. Land with your left leg first, push with your hands, bring the other foot down, and stand up straight. Try to keep a rhythm ("hand, hand, foot, foot").

If you find yourself flopping to one side before you have completed the cartwheel, you could try practicing beside a wall — this will discourage your legs from going down in front of or behind you.

HOW TO WRITE A LETTER

1. Start with your address at the top right side of the page. Below it, to the left, put the name and address of the person you are writing to. Put the day's date on the line below that, on the left-hand side of the page.

2. Below and to the left, address the person you are writing to. If you know the person well, start with "Dear Dad" (or similar). If the letter is more formal, start with "Dear Mr./Mrs. Smith," or "Dear Sirs/Dear Sir or Madam."

3. Leave a line blank and on the next line, starting at the left, begin writing your letter. Remember to use paragraphs and always check your spelling — get into the habit of using a dictionary. Whether you are typing or writing by hand, make sure the page is nicely spaced.

4. End your letter on a new line to the left side of the page. If it is to a parent or friend, close your letter with: "Love," "With love," or even "Hugs and kisses." If it is to someone you don't know quite as well, leave it at: "With affectionate greetings" or "With best wishes." "With best wishes" can also be used to finish more formal letters, often followed by sign-offs, such as:
- to someone whose name you know: "Yours sincerely,"
- to someone whose name you do not know (i.e., Sir or Madam): "Sincerely."

5. When addressing the envelope, make sure it is clear and readable, and use a different line for each separate part of the address.

HOW TO BUNNY HOP

Being able to hop with your bike and lift both wheels off the ground is a great skill.

Start by hopping the bike over a line on the ground, then move on to using a thin stick, and then steadily increase your hopping height. Don't forget to wear knee pads, elbow pads, gloves, and a fitted helmet for safety.

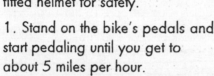

1. Stand on the bike's pedals and start pedaling until you get to about 5 miles per hour.

2. Lean the upper part of your body over the handlebars, keeping your weight centered.

3. Get your pedals level, so that your feet are parallel to the ground.

4. As you prepare for your hop, press down on the handlebars and pedals. Push your feet down, back, and then up, in one motion.

5. As you move your feet upward, lessen the pressure of your feet and hands slightly but maintain contact between yourself and the bike. Crouch down on the bike and hop into the air.

6. Land as lightly as you can, taking the impact in your arms and legs, not your back.

HOW TO SHAKE OFF A TAIL

"A tail" is slang for a person secretly following someone else to observe where they go and what they do. Your first task is to find out if you are being followed, and if so, by whom. Your second task is to lose them.

Most amateur tails will follow behind you, trying not to be spotted.

1. If you think you are being followed, occasionally stop as you walk around — perhaps to tie a shoelace, look for something in your pocket, admire something in a store window, and so on. Casually scan people behind you — possibly on the other side of the road — and make a rough note of anyone within distance, especially such things as height, color of clothes, type of coat, etc.; also look for anyone you recognize from earlier on in your day. Stop again after a few hundred yards and take a casual glance around as before — is anyone still there?

2. If there is, continue walking. Use your ingenuity. Stop and look in shop windows, or pause to admire a shiny car or van (choose dark-colored ones) — you can use the reflection on these surfaces to see who's behind you. Or pull out a comb and peer into the side mirror of a parked car or motorbike, as though about to comb your hair — is there anyone whose reflection you recognize? If you're still not sure, try dawdling along and then suddenly stop dead (as though you'd suddenly forgotten something really important) and let everyone else walk past you — is there anyone who has also stopped and who seems to be waiting?

3. Once you are certain you are being followed, make a note of what the person looks like. At the same time, make a plan for losing him or her.

4. When you are out of sight, change your own distinguishing features: If you're wearing a coat, take it off; if you're carrying a bag, hide it in your shirt; if you're wearing a hat, stuff it in your pocket, or if you've got a hat in a pocket, put it on.

5. Speed up: Do this not by quickening your pace, but by lengthening your strides — if your pace is 1 foot long, and you lengthen it to 16 inches, in 100 yards you'll have traveled an extra $33\frac{1}{3}$ yards.

6. Try to shake the tail: Enter a large shop and immediately leave by another exit; go down a narrow alley and, while out of sight of your tail, sprint around a corner and double back on your tracks, resuming your normal pace once you're back on a main street. Jump on a bus just as it's about to shut its doors — the possibilities are endless.

7. As a last resort, hide: Wait until you're out of your tail's sight; the moment you are, duck into a deep doorway, crouch down behind a parked car or a low wall, duck into the hallway of a large building — in short, anywhere that he or she will hurry past hoping to catch up with you again. Remember, your tail will be anxious not to lose you, and in that state of mind will probably overlook something right under his or her nose.

8. If you feel you are truly in danger, don't hesitate to alert an adult or the police.

HOW TO LASSO LIKE A COWBOY

To make your lasso, you will need about 33 feet of stiff cord (the rope), a large needle, and some thin string.

Take one end of the rope and make a small loop. It needs to be big enough for the rope to pass through it easily — but not much bigger than that. Instead of tying, sew the end to the rope with the string to make a permanent loop at one end. This loop is called a honda.

Honda

Loop

Preparing and throwing the lasso:

1. Position yourself in front of your target, a post or tree stump, for instance. Pull the loose end of the rope through the honda. Stop when you have about 10 feet left to feed through. This will be the loop you use to snare your target.

2. Coil the loose end of the rope and hold it in one hand. Leave about 5 feet between the coil and the loop to allow you to swing your lasso.

3. Hold the loop end of the rope in your free hand, about 8 inches from where the loop runs through the honda.

4. Spin the lasso over your head with clockwise turns of your hand, tracing a circle in the air. Let your wrist act as

an axle, and swing the rope as if it were a wheel spinning horizontally around your wrist and over your head.

5. When you feel ready to lasso your target, give a quick step forward, bring your hand forward and down to the level of your shoulder, let it stretch to a full arm's length without interrupting the swinging motion of the loop, and let it go at your target. The loop should sail straight at your target without losing its circular form.

Warning: Don't ever try to lasso a person or pet. Practice your lasso skills on an inanimate object, like a chair.

HOW TO MAKE A VOLCANO

This is a messy project and needs space, so if you can, make it outdoors or cover your work area with newspaper.

You will need: cardboard, a funnel, modeling clay (brown and red are best), an empty plastic bottle, baking soda, red food coloring, liquid soap, and vinegar.

1. Place the plastic bottle on the piece of cardboard.

2. Make a volcano shape around the bottle with the modeling clay. Use brown clay for the base, and red clay for the rim to look like hot lava. If you can't find red clay, color a small amount of the brown with the food coloring.

3. Use a funnel to pour 1 tablespoon of baking soda, a few drops of red food coloring, and a few drops of liquid soap into the bottle.

4. Pour in ¼ cup of vinegar, stand back, and watch the volcano erupt.

HOW TO FIND ORION

The constellation Orion, the Hunter, can be seen all over the world because it lies on the celestial equator. Even if you haven't identified them in the night sky, you may have heard of some of the stars that make up this constellation, including Rigel and Betelgeuse.

1. Look toward the south if you are in the Northern Hemisphere, the north if you are in the Southern Hemisphere.

2. Find Orion's belt — three stars.

3. Look for Orion's knee to the lower right — it's the bright star, Rigel.

4. Locate the orange-red star, Betelgeuse, at the upper left from the belt, often called "Beetlejuice."

Betelgeuse

Rigel

HOW TO BEND IT LIKE BECKHAM

1. Approach the soccer ball at an angle. Place your standing foot (rather than your kicking foot) close to the ball, facing the direction you want the ball to go. Start by practicing this as you go to kick the ball.

2. Once you're comfortable with this, try to "bend it." If you kick with your right foot, to send the ball from right to left, strike the bottom half of the right-hand side with the inside, top half of your foot. To curve the ball from left to right, strike the bottom half of the left side of the ball with the outside of your foot. (Reverse these moves if you kick with your left foot.) To swerve a ball with the outside of your foot, strike across the ball.

HOW TO MAKE A WATER CLOCK

You will need four paper cups all the same size, four pins, a sturdy piece of cardboard, a glass jar at least as big as the cup, a narrow strip of paper, glue, a stopwatch, and a pencil.

1. Use a pin to prick a hole in the bottom of each cup.

2. Pin the five cups to the cardboard, one under the other. Leave a three-finger gap between each cup.

3. Glue the strip of paper vertically to the glass jar and put the jar under the bottom cup.

4. Fill the top cup with water and check that it drips through each cup into the jar at the bottom.

5. OK? Then do it again, using the same amount of water, but this time start your stopwatch the moment you start pouring.

6. At intervals of five minutes, mark the water level on the paper on your jar.

7. When all the water has dripped into the jar, you can use this "clock" to keep track of time.

HOW TO TANGLE YOUR FRIEND'S BRAIN

Tell your friend that you can tangle his mind so that he won't know which finger is which. If he accepts your challenge, give him the following instructions:

- Hold your arms in front of you, and cross them at the wrists.
- Twist your palms so that they are facing each other, and interlock your fingers.
- Bring your hands to your stomach while turning your interlocked fingers upward toward your face.

Once your friend's hands are in position, ask him to try and lift one of his fingers. The third and fourth fingers are the most difficult, so start with these for maximum effect. Make sure you only point to the finger you want him to move— touching it can spoil the trick. Watch his puzzled face as he keeps lifting up the wrong finger.

HOW TO STUMP A KNOW-IT-ALL

"Did you know that your brain's 80 percent water?"

(This is a fact, not an insult.)

HOW TO BE A MATH MASTER

1. Ask a friend to think of a three-digit number. The only condition is that the first digit and the last digit must differ by more than one — for example, 364 would not work because there is a difference of only one between the first and last digits (3 and 4).

2. Your friend might need a calculator — you, of course, do not. Now tell your friend to reverse the number. Let's say he or she chose 469 — reversing it would be 964.

3. Now tell your friend to subtract the smaller number from the larger (964 − 469 = 495). All this is done without your knowing what any of the numbers are.

4. Tell your friend to now take the result of this subtraction (495 in our example) and reverse it (594), and then to add the result and its reverse together.

5. Your turn now. You announce the answer: 1089.

You will be right every time!

HOW TO WARM UP YOUR FEET

Sprinkle a pinch of ground cayenne pepper into your socks. It will warm your feet without burning them. But be sure that any cuts, blisters, and scratches on your feet are covered with a bandage, and be very careful not to allow the pepper to touch your eyes, or the nose and mouth area, as it might sting or at least feel uncomfortably hot.

HOW TO CLIMB A ROPE

To most people, a long rope with no knots to grip looks impossible to climb. Here's how to escape the gym teacher and wriggle up the rope like a boa constrictor:

1. Stand in front of the rope and reach up with both arms — they should be well above your head, but slightly bent at the elbows to give you the necessary leverage.

2. Grasp the rope and pull yourself up. As you do so, cross your legs around the rope and grip it between your thighs and again between your feet.

3. Reach up again, one arm at a time. Pull yourself up with your hands while using the grip between your feet and thighs to push up.

HOW TO MAKE A BOOMERANG

Boomerangs do not have to be single-angled pieces of wood. They were traditionally that shape because they were made from bent pieces of wood. If you make one out of cardboard, an X-shape boomerang is far more effective.

You will need: cardboard, a ruler, scissors, glue or a stapler, and colored markers (to decorate).

1. Measure and cut two lengths of cardboard 8 x 1 ¼ inches. Make sure the sides of each length are parallel and that the two lengths are identical to each other. Cut the eight corners so that they are nicely rounded.

2. Fold up the end of each wing about ¾ inch from the tip, to make a rough right angle.

3. Lay one piece across the other to form an X, crossing them in the center and at right angles. Glue or staple them together at the center. Decorate your creation. Always use your boomerang outdoors and never throw it toward a person or animal.

4. To throw, hold your boomerang vertically by one of its blades so the folded tips bend toward you. Raise your arm and throw it with a quick snap of your wrist, using just a little force.

5. If it doesn't work after several tries, adjust the folded ends. You could also try placing four pea-sized blobs of putty on the underside of each wing about three-quarters of the length from the center. Soon it'll whiz back to you every time.

HOW TO DOWSE FOR WATER

Dowsing is a way of locating something that is hidden. A person — the dowser — using a rod, stick, or other device known as a dowsing rod or "wishing rod," can determine the exact location of such things as underground water, buried treasure, oil, lost objects, and even people. Since the art of dowsing has never been scientifically proven, it is considered a type of divination.

Traditional dowsing rods were made from forked hazel branches, although the wood of apple, beech, and alder are said to work as well. Alternatively, L-shaped copper or iron rods are used — or, unmystical as it sounds, wire coat hangers.

To make dowsing rods out of wire hangers, you need the long horizontal wire (the part over which you might drape a pair of pants) and about 4 inches of one angled side. Ask an adult to help you take two hangers and cut from them this angled length using a pair of wire cutters. Bend each of the short sides out a little to form a right angle or L-shape. The shorter end is the handle: Over each handle, fit half a plastic drinking straw to form a sleeve (this allows the rod to swivel freely without being affected by your hand).

To dowse with your L-shaped rods, hold a rod in each hand, horizontally in front of you. When you're over water the rods will cross each other, apparently moving of their own accord, pointing toward the spot where the water can be found.

HOW TO TAKE A JUMP SHOT

1. Start with both feet flat on the floor. With your body facing the basket, crouch down low — this will give you the momentum to jump.

2. Start your jump. Make sure you can see the rim of the hoop. Your shooting hand should cup the ball and point toward the basket, while your other hand can gently guide the shot, loosely holding the side of the ball.

3. Keep your elbows in and your eyes on the back of the rim. Bend the wrist of your shooting hand backward, the ball resting on the pads of your fingers.

4. As you spring off the ground, extend your arms, raising the ball smoothly in one fluid motion.

5. At the top of the jump, snap your wrist forward and let go of the ball.

6. At the end of the shot, when the ball flies through the hoop, your fingers should be pointing down to the floor.

HOW TO MAKE FIRE

1. Ask an adult to help you with this activity.

2. Rapidly twirling a dry twig around inside a hole in a piece of wood or a dead tree trunk will produce enough heat to light dry moss on fire.

3. Cutting a slot into a piece of bamboo and wearing down this slot with another piece of bamboo will work off fragments of the wood. The friction will set these shavings on fire.

4. Striking a stone against a flint will create sparks that, if they fall onto dry moss, can set it on fire.

5. If it is bright and sunny, you can set paper, dry moss, or grass on fire by holding a magnifying glass over it and drawing it upward until the circle of sunlight the glass makes on the area is a tiny bright point. Hold it there and a tiny curl of smoke will soon appear, and then flames.

HOW TO SPEED-READ

When you read, it is not necessary to look at every letter of a word to know what the word is; you don't even have to see the word in detail, as you know by its shape and length and by its context (the meaning of the rest of the sentence in which it appears) what it is. To speed-read you have to be able to scan the lines you are reading. The brain soon learns which words are the important ones and also learns to take in several words together.

To speed up your reading, run your finger along beneath each line you read. Gradually increase the speed of your finger and you'll find your reading speeds up, too. Don't go too fast at first, though, or you won't take in what you're reading.

To improve your speed-reading, use a newspaper, as the columns are narrower than book pages. Draw a line right down the center of a column. Now try to read each line of words without moving your eyes from the beginning to the end of the line but by looking at its center. You'll find that, with practice, your eyes are taking in a complete line at a time — and if you continue, you'll find that your brain starts doing the same and you can fully understand what you're reading. After a while, don't draw the line and you'll soon be able to read a newspaper column just by running your eyes down the center.

Avoid saying the words to yourself and going back over something you've just read. Doing so will slow you down.

HOW TO SURVIVE AN EARTHQUAKE

Fortunately the great majority of the earthquakes that are occurring around us nearly all the time are so slight that only seismographs register them. Stronger earthquakes, however, can cause a great deal of damage.

1. If you are indoors and have time, turn off all gas- and fire-related equipment (a gas stove, for instance). Stay indoors. Drop down to the floor and take cover under a sturdy table or desk. Hold on to it and, if necessary, move with it. If there are no suitable pieces of furniture, stand in a doorway. Keep clear of windows, glass, fireplaces, and

heavy furniture or appliances. Stay put until the shaking stops and it's safe to move.

2. If you're outside, get out into the open. Stay away from buildings, trees, power lines, bridges, high walls, and rocks.

3. If you're in a car, urge everyone to stay in the vehicle. Ask the driver to keep the car away from traffic, bridges, overpasses and tunnels, trees, lampposts, power lines, and road signs, and to stop the car where it seems safe.

4. After the shaking has stopped, check for any injured people and make sure they're as comfortable and safe as possible; check for hazards — fire, water leakages, damaged structures — turn off power supplies if a gas leak is suspected or electrical wiring is damaged, and clean up dangerous spills. Only use the telephone for emergencies and keep listening to the radio. Be prepared for aftershocks and even tidal waves.

The Richter scale measures an earthquake's strength:

1–3	Generally not felt but recorded on seismographs
3–4	Felt, but damage very rare
4–5	Widely felt, some local damage, not significant
5–6	Damage to poorly constructed buildings
6–7	Destructive — a fair amount of damage
7–8	Major — serious damage over large areas
8–9	Great — widespread destruction and loss of life
9–plus	Rare — causes great destruction over huge area

HOW TO LOCATE A THUNDERSTORM

Water droplets colliding inside storm clouds cause electrons to move so quickly that a large electrical spark is created. This is lightning. The air along its path is heated so intensely and expands so much that it creates a very loud noise – thunder. But although lightning and thunder occur together, we see the lightning some time before we hear the thunder because the speed of light is about a million times that of sound.

It is possible to estimate how far away a thunderstorm is by counting the number of seconds between the lightning flash and the thunderclap. Divide what you get by five and that will give you the approximate distance in miles.

HOW TO MAKE A SPACE DART

1. Take an 8¹/₂ x 11 inch piece of paper and crease it along the center, by folding it in half along the length then opening it out again. Fold the two edges into the center crease you have just made.

2. Fold the top corners diagonally to the center crease to make two right-angled triangles.

3. Fold back the two lower flaps of the dart along the dotted lines to make two large, folded-back triangles.

4. Fold in the two top corners along the dotted lines.

5. Fold the dart in half along the central crease.

6. Fold down the tops of the dart to create wings. The crisper you can get your folds the more accurate your dart will be.

7. Your space dart is ready to launch. Hold it steady between your thumb and your index finger, with the rest of your fingers tucked under. Pull your arm back, then snap your wrist forward to release the dart and send it flying.

Tip. The space dart is a fast, accurate flier. If you are in a speed contest, throw it as hard as you can. If you are in an accuracy contest, throw it a little slower.

HOW TO ROW A BOAT

It is a good idea not to go off alone in a boat — take an adult with you. Make sure you are prepared — that you are both wearing life jackets and that the boat is dry and in good condition.

1. Sit with your back to the bow (the front of the boat) and your feet against the foot board, your legs slightly bent at the knee. Place an oar in each oarlock — the U-shaped metal fittings that fit into holes in the boat's side to hold the oars.

2. Your companion should get into the boat and sit at the back — that is, on the stern thwart. Get him or her to push the boat off from the dock or jetty so that it drifts out.

3. With your arms straight out in front of you, hold the oar handles with your wrists dropped so that the oar blades are parallel to and just above the surface of the water. Keep your back straight and look directly in front of you, which, when you're rowing, is over the stern (the back of the boat).

4. Lower the oar blades into the water and, at the same time, straighten your wrists — this will set the blades at right angles to the surface as they enter.

5. Lean back and bring the oar handles toward your chest, completing the stroke by bending your arms. Your weight, and the effort of your legs, more than the strength of your arms, pull the blades through the water, making the boat

move in the opposite direction, so you are effectively going backward.

6. As the stroke ends, lift the blades from the water, straighten your arms, and lean forward again — this will bring the blades back to the starting point.

7. Lower the blades into the water and take another stroke, and so on. The hardest strokes are the first six or seven; once the boat is actually moving, less effort is needed to keep it traveling at the same pace.

8. Pulling harder on one oar will make the boat turn away from that side — i.e., if you pull on your right oar, the boat will move toward your left (which is to the boat's right, since you're facing backward).

9. To slow or stop the boat, drop the blades into the water and brace yourself against them — the flat blades will act as brakes. To move the boat backward, hold that position and then push against the oar handles, so that the blades move through the water in the opposite direction. As the blades near the bow, lift them out of the water, lean back, and drop them in again to take another stroke — in effect, rowing in reverse.

If for any reason the boat capsizes and you end up in the water — don't panic! Your life jacket will keep you afloat. Stay close to the boat until help arrives or until you and your companion can push it to the dock by holding on to one side and kicking with your legs. You can climb back in provided your companion is holding on to the other side as you do so, to counterbalance your weight.

HOW TO TELL WHICH WAY IS NORTH

You will need:
a wristwatch with hands,
set to the correct local
time. You need to be
able to see the sun (even
if it's shining through a
cloud). Most important of
all, you also need to
know that the sun rises in
the east and sets in the
west; and that at 12
noon in the Northern
Hemisphere it is due
south (in the Southern
Hemisphere it's due north).

Northern Hemisphere

1. Holding the watch horizontally, aim the hour hand at the sun. Then divide the angle between the position of the hour hand and the 12 on the watch face (or the 1 during Daylight Saving Time) — the line that follows that angle is the north-south line. Since you know the position of the sun at noon, and you know the time, you can then work out which way is north and which way is south.

2. If you have a digital watch, draw a watch face on a piece of paper, mark the 12, and then draw in the hour hand in the position for the time shown on your digital. Next aim the hour hand in the drawing at the sun and follow the procedure for a watch with hands (technically termed an analog watch).

3. If you are in the southern hemisphere, aim the 12 on the watch face at the sun and find the north-south line by bisecting the angle between the hour hand and 12. Remember that in this hemisphere, the sun will be due north at noon; otherwise, exactly the same principles apply as for the northern hemisphere.

HOW TO GET AN EGG INTO A BOTTLE

You will need: a peeled, hard-boiled egg, a glass bottle with an opening slightly smaller than the egg, and matches. Ask an adult for help.

1. To hard-boil an egg, put it in a saucepan, cover it with water, and let it simmer for 8 to 10 minutes. Then put it in cold water and leave it for at least another 10 minutes to cool down. When the egg has cooled, tap it gently until the shell cracks. Peel it carefully.

2. Light three matches and drop them in the bottle at the same time. Quickly place the egg, pointed side down, in the bottle opening.

3. When the matches go out, the air inside the bottle will cool and the egg will slowly move into the bottle.

4. To get the egg out, hold the bottle upside-down so that the egg is near the opening. Blow hard into the bottle with your mouth tight against the opening. The egg will vibrate, but then act as a seal, trapping air inside. Point the bottle away from yourself and watch the egg fly out.

HOW TO TIE A KNOT WITH ONE HAND

1. Drape the string over your hand.

2. Bend your hand, and with your first and second fingers, pick up the string that is hanging behind your hand.

3. Flick your wrist down, so the string on top of your hand slides off the front of your fingers.

And presto, a knot.

HOW TO RIDE A UNICYCLE

1. Get two friends to stand on either side of you and get up on the unicycle with your arms around their shoulders. Check that the unicycle is the correct height by sitting on the seat and placing one foot on a pedal at the lowest point. You should be able to reach that pedal with your leg very slightly bent.

2. Sit up straight and look straight ahead. Your weight should be on the seat, not on the pedals. Rock the pedals to get a sense of balance, and then bring the pedals around so that they're parallel with the ground.

3. Still holding on to your helpers, pedal a half-turn, then stop. Do this a few times before going on to pedal full turns. Doing lots of half-turns (from pedals level to pedals level again) is harder than continuous pedaling, but keeps you in control of the movement.

4. Switch from holding on to your helpers' shoulders to holding their wrists, and then to holding the wrist of just one helper.

5. Let go of both helpers and switch to using a wall instead. Pedal a half-turn forward, sliding your hand along the wall. Build this up into a whole turn, two turns, and so on until you are comfortable sliding along the wall with only a very light hold on it.

6. To turn the unicycle, swivel your body and the unicycle in the direction you want to go, but be careful to avoid leaning to the side.

HOW TO DRAW A CARTOON

If you can draw a basic face shape, it is very easy to adjust certain features to give each of your cartoons a different personality. Start with a basic oval, then add other circles for the nose and eyes. Then simply decorate with different-shaped mouths, and try moving the eyeballs or eyebrows, or adding hair or glasses. See what expressions you can create. You will soon begin to build a library of faces with different and hilarious personalities.

HOW TO WRITE A LIMERICK

A limerick is a poem with five lines. It always has the same rhyming pattern and rhythm. The first, second, and fifth lines usually have eight syllables each, and the final syllables of each of these lines rhyme. The middle lines both have five or six syllables and a different rhyme.

1. Begin by picking a boy's or girl's name and write an eight-syllable line with that name at the end. For example: "There once was a young man named Matt. . . ."

2. Make a list of words that rhyme with the last syllable in the first line — for instance, hat, cat, fat, sat, pat, rat. Now write a second eight-syllable line ending with one of your rhyming words. For example: "Whose pet was a rat in a hat."

3. Now think of a story for your character and write two five-syllable lines with words that rhyme at the end. For example: "The rat said, 'You know, / The hat has to go.'"

4. For the final line, which will be eight syllables long, think of a resolution for your story. Go back to your list of rhyming words and be as silly as you want. "A cat wears a hat, not a rat."

HOW TO MILK A COW

1. Secure the cow.

2. Clean your hands and the cow's teats with soap water.

3. Put a dollop of udder cream on your hands.

4. Take the base of the cow's teat firmly between the last three fingers of your left hand.

5. Squeeze the teat and the udder at the same time.

6. Do not jerk or pull — this will irritate the cow and can cause injury.

7. With your right hand, take the base of another teat firmly between the last three fingers and repeat as above.

8. Proceed quickly, but gently, with each hand until the supply of milk finishes.

Warning: Always approach a cow slowly. Don't make any sudden movements or you might get stepped on or kicked.

HOW TO DRIBBLE A BASKETBALL

In basketball, dribbling is the only legal way to move with the ball. It involves bouncing the ball with one hand so that it bounces back to your fingers while you're running.

Use dribbling to move the ball forward, to dodge around the player marking you, to get into a good position to pass or shoot, and to escape from a strong defense.

Keep your head up and your eyes focused on the court at all times. Don't look at the ball.

Spread your fingers over the top of the ball and push it down toward the floor by flexing your wrist.

Keep your hand positioned over the top of the ball so that its rebound is accurate. Make sure you control your push enough to keep the ball bouncing at waist height.

Don't let the ball slap against your palm. Always touch the ball with your fingers, and use your wrists to control the movement of the ball.

Keep you knees bent to help your balance and always bounce on the balls of your feet as you move forward.

Tip. Don't stop dribbling until you know what you're going to do with the ball. Once you touch the ball with both hands, you must either pass or shoot the ball.

HOW TO KEEP PEOPLE IN SUSPENSE

A "cliff-hanger" is anything in a story, article, radio or TV show, or movie that leaves the listener, reader, or viewer in suspense — for instance, the hero is left hanging from a cliff, in deadly danger of losing his life. It is a trick used to keep people's attention — by being kept in suspense, they want to know more.

You can use similar tricks to become the best teller (or writer) of jokes, stories, and even speeches, and hold your audience in suspense:

1. Don't give too much away too early. Quickly ending an account with something like "Suddenly shots rang out and they all died. The End." leaves people disappointed and frustrated.

2. Never rush. Drag the tale out (but don't go so slowly that it becomes boring). Pause occasionally — this often makes people say, "Keep going!" or "What happened next?"

3. Change direction. Just as you get to a good part, say something like "Meanwhile, as the phantom bus bore down on us, Gran was baking a cake at home. . . ."

4. Break off your story occasionally. "Then suddenly a huge black shape appeared in front of him and he — oh, there goes the bell. I'll finish later."

5. Leave the best part for the end, but build up the drama bit by bit.

HOW TO KEEP A SECRET JOURNAL

1. Make sure that your journal is special to you. You might want to cover a blank pad with paper, fabric, or photos.

2. Don't feel that you have to write something every day.

3. Focus on the details of your day: who you saw, what you did, where you went, and how you felt.

4. Don't hold back. Write boldly.

5. If you are writing sensational material about people you know, disguise their identities with code names.

6. It may help to address your entries to an imaginary person.

7. Keep it somewhere safe and away from prying eyes.

8. Just to be extra sure that no one will ever read it, write something like MY BOOK OF ALGEBRA on the cover.

HOW TO PROVE YOU'RE NOT BIGHEADED

So people say you've got a big head and that you think you are the best at everything? How do you prove them wrong? Simple — you put your head through a playing card.

1. Fold an old playing card down the middle lengthwise and crease it hard along the fold.

2. With a pair of scissors, make eight evenly spaced cuts along the folded edge, but make sure you stop before you reach the far edge.

3. Turn the card around and make seven cuts along the open edge, in between the first set of cuts. Don't cut through the folded edge.

4. Flatten out the card and cut carefully along the crease from A to B. Now open out the card gently into a large, ragged ring, and put your head through it.

HOW TO SEND A MESSAGE BY SEMAPHORE

Semaphore is a code that uses different arm positions to represent each of the letters of the alphabet. To start a message, cross your arms in front of you with your elbows straight and hands pointing to the ground. This position means "Attention" or "End of Message." Spell out your message letter by letter using the positions below. The black flag shows the position of your left arm, and the white flag, the position of your right arm.

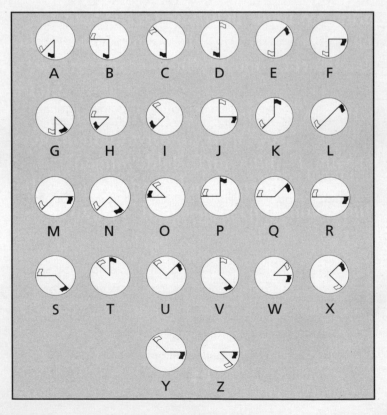

HOW TO FIND FOSSILS AND TREASURE

Wherever you are, you may be standing on a fossil: perhaps bones, teeth, eggs, frozen mammoth flesh, or fossilized fur. And there are other kinds of fascinating treasure to discover, too, such as ancient artifacts, old coins, jewelry, and pottery.

You don't have to be an archaeologist or paleontologist to uncover the remains of ancient life — you just need to be observant, patient, and lucky.

Where to look:

1. **Beaches:** Look under rocks as well as in the sand, there could be fossils.

2. **Riverbanks:** Check under stones and along the water's edge. Shallow streambeds are also worth investigating.

3. **Cliffs:** Erosion might uncover some super fossils (or Stone Age carvings), which you could find either in the cliff face or at the foot of the cliff.

4. **Quarries:** These are good places to look, where stone and earth has been dug up to use for building (but do observe safety precautions).

5. **Farmland:** It's worth looking in farmland, too, especially fields where plowing might have turned up the earth and all kinds of treasures that have been buried for years, or even centuries, may have come to the surface.

You will need tools to help unearth your fossils and treasure. Use a brush to gently remove any sand or soil, a small trowel to dig around your discovery, and a hammer and chisel if you are in a rocky area. Take paper towels with you to wrap your fossils, a camera to record your discoveries, and plastic bags so you can carry them to the museum!

HOW TO TEST YOUR TELEPATHIC POWERS

Prepare six flash cards. Each one should show a very simple picture. Here are some suggestions of what you could draw: a square, a triangle, a star, a circle, a wavy line, and a spiral.

Sit back-to-back with a friend and decide who will be the sender and who will be the receiver.

The sender shuffles the flash cards. Then one by one the sender takes the top card in the pile, shouts, "Go" and concentrates really hard on "sending" the image to the receiver.

The receiver has a pencil and paper and draws whatever comes into his mind. When all the cards have been "sent," compare the flash cards sent by the sender to the pictures drawn by the receiver in each instance. Look for similarities. For example, a triangle may be telepathically received as the sail of a boat.

HOW TO BE THE BEST ALL AROUND THE WORLD

If you know many languages, you can be the best around the world . . . or at least people will think you are!

English	I am the best.
French	Je suis le meilleur.
Russian	Ya velikiy.
Spanish	Soy lo mejor.
Italian	Sono il migliore.
Urdu	Mãi sab se achã.
Portuguese	Sou o melhor.
German	Ich bin das Beste.
Swedish	Jag är bäst.
Danish	Jeg er den bedst.
Greek	E-me o kaliteros.
Polish	Jestem wspaniały.
Arabic	Ana Al'aadham.
Mandarin	Wǒ shi zuì hǎo de.
Hindi	Mãi sab se achã.
Swahili	Mimi mbinga ni.
Latin	Optimus sum.

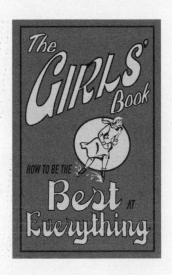